Original title:
The Necklace's Dance

Copyright © 2025 Creative Arts Management OÜ
All rights reserved.

Author: Harrison Blake
ISBN HARDBACK: 978-1-80586-194-2
ISBN PAPERBACK: 978-1-80586-666-4

The Allure of a Bright Horizon

In a shop with treasures bright,
A jewel caught her eye,
She spun and twirled with delight,
As if she could fly.

With a wink, she donned the fake,
Feeling fancy and grand,
But slipping on a cake,
She landed with a thud on sand!

The crowd roared with laughter,
As she made her grand show,
That bling a happy disaster,
In the spotlight's glow.

With every hum and shimmy,
She dazzled, fell, and pranced,
A comedic frenzy,
In glitter, she romanced.

Prisms of Wonder

In a box of gleams and dreams,
The sparkles giggle and tease,
They twirl like dancers on the floor,
With laughter carried in the breeze.

They pop and bounce like joyful kids,
Each facet a story to share,
A riot of colors, a party of light,
Spreading joy everywhere.

Gems of Glittering Twilight

Underneath the moonlit sky,
The stones begin their cheeky play,
With winks and nods, they pile up high,
At twilight's call, they steal away.

A ruby trips on an emerald's foot,
While sapphires sport a silly hat,
They giggle and jump, what a hoot,
In a playful sparkly spat!

Twirling in Silver Shadows

In shadows where the moonlight flares,
The gems get silly, hold on tight,
They whirl and spin without a care,
Creating laughter in the night.

A diamond twirls with a playful leap,
As lanterns dance in playful rows,
Their merry jests in shadows creep,
Lightfooted, they strike funny poses.

Elegance in Motion

With a wink of gold and a flash of blue,
They strut their stuff like kings and queens,
A comical show, oh what a view,
Adorned in laughter, draped in sheen.

With every twist, they jest and prance,
In a shimmering ballet so divine,
They make us clap, they make us dance,
Grinning wide, they steal the shine.

Artistry of Adornments Unfolding

In a box of gems, the chaos reigns,
A pearl jumps out, it twirls and trains,
The rubies laugh in a tangled mess,
While laughter echoes, oh what a dress!

A charm once bright, now lost its shine,
Dances with glee, 'Is this still mine?'
An earring spins, a dizzy affair,
It twirls like mad in the heavy air!

Where Sparkle Meets Serenity

A brooch sits still, playing coy and shy,
While a bracelet sings, oh my oh my!
The necklaces giggle, drop with flair,
In the quiet tune, a jazzy air.

A ring jumps high, says, 'Catch me if you can!'
While the bangle sways, saying, 'Yes, I'm the man!'
Together they whirl, an eclectic banter,
Jewelry shindig, a fashion canter!

Rhythms of the Gilded Heart

Gold chains snapping, they tap their feet,
While diamond studs prepare for a beat,
They clink and clatter, a shiny surprise,
Under the moon, they twinkle and rise.

A choker squeaks, 'I'm still in style!'
A pendant replies, with a wiggly smile,
Together they leap, into whimsical bliss,
Each jewel a partner, twirling like this!

Celestial Glimmers Amidst Shadows

Sparkles shattered in a playful spree,
Where shadows dance with glee and decree,
A comet of gems leaves a trail so fine,
While laughter wraps round, like wisteria vine.

A star-shaped bracelet does a little jig,
The moonstone winks, feeling rather big,
In a cosmic ballet of shimmer and twirl,
They glow through the night, in a jazzy swirl!

Wings of Sparkles Framed in Time

In a whirlwind of twirls, they leap and spin,
With laughter and jewels, oh where to begin!
Each step a giggle, a pirouette bold,
As sparkles fly free, like stories untold.

A wink from a star, they dance in the light,
While shadows and secrets come out of the night.
Chasing the echoes of dreams wrapped in gold,
Their hearts beat together, a sight to behold.

Glistening Tapestry of Whimsy

In a tapestry bright, with colors a-swish,
They prance like young fairies, fulfilling a wish.
Each thread tells a joke, a tale full of cheer,
With giggles of joy that the world longs to hear.

As ribbons entwine in a comedic whirl,
A twinkle of mischief makes every boy twirl.
With flashes of silver, they shimmer and sway,
In this funny ballet, they frolic away.

Caprice of Adorned Souls

With hats on their heads and feathers so grand,
They prance in the park, making life quite unplanned.
Each ornament jangles with every delight,
A caper of chaos through day and through night.

In shoes that are bright, they stomp and they slide,
Creating a symphony, a foolish joyride.
With laughter as lanterns, they twinkle and beam,
Making the world feel like a whimsical dream.

Mosaic of Glittered Memories

A mosaic of giggles sprinkled with spark,
As memories dance, lighting up the dark.
With glittered confetti, they fly through the air,
Creating a joyous, whimsical fair.

In circles and swirls, they flip and they flop,
Each moment a treasure, a fizzy pop!
With time as their partner, they bounce to a tune,
Forever in laughter, beneath the bright moon.

A Medley of Luminescent Wishes

In a world of twinkling dreams,
A lady lost her midnight beams.
She danced with pearls upon her dress,
Swirling laughter, oh what a mess!

A spin, a twirl, oh what a sight,
Beads flew off into the night.
"Catch those charms!" her friends exclaimed,
While she just giggled, unashamed.

With every step, her hopes took flight,
As sequins shimmered in moonlight.
Yet one wee step, she slipped and flopped,
The brilliant show? It simply stopped!

And as the crowd roared with delight,
She blushed and bowed, her cheeks so bright.
In laughter's weave, she'll find her grace,
A medley of wishes fills the space.

Choreography of Gleaming Hues

Her heels clicked like a castanet,
In glimmering hues, she took the bet.
With each bold move, the crowd they cheered,
Until her wig took flight, they jeered!

A pirouette turned into a dance,
As glitter marched off, not a chance!
Through frills and thrills, her spirit soared,
Yet somewhere, jewels were ignored.

With every spin, a giggle slipped,
As she unraveled, her friends just quipped,
"Hold onto your jewels, don't lose sight!"
But laughter echoed all through the night.

In this choreography, so absurd,
They found the joy, without a word.
For in this whirl, the heart finds beats,
Amongst scattered gems, laughter repeats.

Treasures Cast in Gossamer Light

She donned her baubles all aglow,
Stepped out with flair, ready to show.
But as she skipped, her earring flew,
"I chase my treasures, who knew?"

With each bright beam, a twinkle burst,
Friends rolled in laughter, oh how they burst!
A necklace danced round her neck like fish,
"Pretty sparkles, come grant my wish!"

Yet one quick twirl, her bracelet snapped,
Like a comet caught in a trap.
They dashed and dove, oh what a sight,
Chasing treasures that took flight!

In gossamer glow, they all did prance,
For every stumble was just a chance.
With every giggle, their spirits bright,
The night shone on in wild delight.

Silent Stories of Shining Mystique

In a room where whispers gleam,
A lady danced, lost in a dream.
Her jewels whispered tales untold,
And laughter spilled like liquid gold.

With every step, her charm did sway,
But oh dear! That pendant's gone astray!
She giggled loud, then ran to find,
Silent stories wrapped in her mind.

Her pearls did roll like tiny suns,
Escaping the dance, oh what fun!
A chase ensued, her friends in tow,
In shiny mischief, their faces aglow.

And as they twirled around the floor,
In shimmering tales, they craved for more.
For in the night, with jewels and cheer,
They danced with joy, the stories clear.

Radiance of a Fashioned Dream

In a world where jewels sway,
The clinks and clatters play.
A brooch attempts a jive,
While the pearls seem quite alive.

Oh, the earrings dangle low,
Twisting with the flow.
Rings try to spin around,
While laughter is the sound.

A tiara claims the crown,
Bowing to no one down.
The bracelet's shimmy-twist,
In glitter, they exist.

One day they'll start a band,
With all their sparkly grand.
As they sway in joyous flair,
They spread style everywhere!

Whispers of Glimmering Beads

Beads chit-chat in a line,
Each whisper a design.
They giggle in the sun,
Oh, how they love to run!

One bead lost its groove,
Said, "I need to move!"
The others laughed out loud,
As they formed a daring crowd.

A glittering shout breaks free,
"Come dance with me, just see!"
Together they parade,
In sparkly escapade.

When evening shadows loom,
They create a joyous room.
In rhythm, they collide,
As laughter can't be denied!

Dancer of Light and Beauty

A lone gemstone takes the floor,
Spinning with a gleam galore.
It waves at every glance,
Inviting all to dance.

The combs are quite ecstatic,
Their moves almost dramatic.
Together, they form a line,
In a shimmering design.

A locket ponders true,
"Shall I join the fun too?"
With a blink and a twirl,
It joins the dizzy whirl.

In a sparkly ruckus, they meet,
Every gem has happy feet.
With a laugh and a twang,
In playful tunes, they sang!

Cascade of Adorned Elegance

A cascade of pearls on high,
Swayed gently, oh my, oh my!
They tumbled down like rain,
Sprinkling laughs like champagne.

The bracelets spin with glee,
Creating quite the spree.
"A twirl! A jump!" they cry,
As the diamonds wink in the sky.

A thrilling clash begins,
As the pendants fight for wins.
They compete with charm and grace,
In this sparking gemstone race!

With glitter flying fast,
Who will outshine, who will last?
In this dance of shades and light,
Laughter reigns supreme tonight!

Pulse of Precious Love

In a swirl of silk and grace,
She stumbled upon a hidden lace.
Her laugh rang out, a joyful sound,
As pearls rolled off the floor and bound.

Dancing shoes did squeak and slide,
While fancy hats took quite a ride.
Oh, the stories that they told,
In every twist and twirl of gold.

With each misstep, a giggly cheer,
The sparkle faded, then drew near.
For love was found in laughter's glow,
While charming blunders stole the show.

So let them twirl, let joy entice,
In every stumble, there's a slice.
Of memories shared, of moments bright,
Hand in hand, they danced through night.

Ornaments of a Forgotten Ball

At midnight, dresses fluffed and twirled,
An elegant mess, the chaos unfurled.
With bows misplaced and ties askew,
The laughter echoed, oh so true.

A lady's hat flew off with flair,
While suitors fumbled for their hair.
Each step taken, a laugh or two,
Ornaments dancing, never knew.

With every mishap, joy would bloom,
Glittering laughter filled the room.
For who needs grace when fun's the quest?
In this strange dance, they were all blessed.

Now here they stand, cheeks rosy bright,
Reminiscing 'bout that crazy night.
Ornaments hung on every frown,
In each shared glance, they never drown.

Beads of Joyful Stories

Once a lady wore a beaded gown,
To shine like stars, but she almost drowned.
In laughter loud, she tripped and spun,
Her radiant joy was second to none.

A dance of beads, a rattling thrill,
Every step sent giggles at will.
Friends gathered 'round, claps like rain,
In this tangled fest, no room for pain.

Stories woven in strands of light,
Each bead a memory, colorful sight.
With every mischief, bonds did grow,
In the playful chaos, love's true glow.

So let them dance with hearts unchained,
In the warmth of laughter, no one feigned.
Stories to cherish, beads won't fall,
Together as one, they've conquered all.

Grace Unveiled in Twinkling Folds

In layers so fine, her dress did flow,
With twinkling folds all set for show.
Yet one wrong move, a slip, a slide,
The grace revealed as friends laughed wide.

Each spin a tale of laughter's art,
As jewels bounced and played their part.
Oh, the stories of gowns gone wild,
In playful chaos, she once was a child.

With giggles escaping as she took a chance,
Every misstep was just another dance.
Twinkling folds held every delight,
Under the stars, all was right.

So here they dance, twirls in delight,
In shimmering folds, they embrace the night.
For in each stumble, love's laughter calls,
Grace unveiled in the joy of their falls.

Harmonies of Dazzling Delights

In the bustling room, gems jive,
A shimmer leads the merry thrive.
Each twinkle has a silly sway,
Bringing laughter in the play.

With every wobble, pearls burst bright,
Knowing well they shine just right.
Twirling skirts and brightened eyes,
What a show, oh what a surprise!

Diamonds chat on jeweled toes,
In giggled tones, the laughter flows.
Rings sing songs of joy and glee,
Oh, what fun it is to see!

Golden lights take center stage,
Even coy foreverage.
They sparkle bright, much to amaze,
In silly, swirling, gemmy ways.

The Jewel's Secret Rhythm

A brooch with a wink, a playful tease,
Shimmies along with grace and ease.
Esmeralda laughs, a cheeky grin,
As rubies spin 'round with a din.

Bangles dance on slender wrists,
Swaying gently, they can't resist.
A chic ballet of color bright,
What a dazzling, comical sight!

Earrings chatter in a playful tune,
Chiming along with the silver moon.
Rings whisper secrets, oh so bold,
And tales of treasure, yet untold.

Bravo! They cheer with every gleam,
In a waltz of jewels, they scheme.
With humor wrapped in glitter's might,
They twinkle until the morning light.

Glint of Enchanted Whims

On a wrist, a bracelet winks,
A playful sound, as laughter sinks.
Gems all jostle for a view,
Making mischief, just like you!

With a clang and a ding, they sway,
Creating jazz in a bright ballet.
Shiny beings cutting loose,
In vibrant, cheerful, gemmy truce!

A tiara spins, oh what a sight,
Making all the jewels feel so light.
Diamonds giggle, emeralds grin,
As they conspire beneath your skin.

With humor wrapped in sparkling flair,
They twist and twirl without a care.
In the moonlight's whispered beams,
They dance like they've got wild dreams.

Embrace of the Shining Echo

In the corner, a sapphire jumps,
Giggling softly, doing lumps.
A pearl's shout breaks the hushed tones,
Tickling everyone on their phones.

Emeralds lurch, trying to bop,
To the rhythm that just won't stop.
Glittering laughter fills the space,
As they whirl in their shining grace.

Rings hold hands, creating chains,
Dancing giddily to their refrains.
Every stone joins the gleeful cheer,
In an embrace that draws them near.

They shine, they jive, what a show,
Humor sparkles, letting all know.
In a playful, cozy glow,
This bejeweled party steals the show!

Jewelry's Silken Waltz

A shiny thing upon her chest,
She flutters like a bird at rest.
With every twirl, it wants to cling,
And makes her feel like a fancy thing.

Laughter echoes in the crowd,
As she shows off, proud and loud.
But alas, it sways too free,
Clinging tight to her jubilee!

Her friends all laugh, their eyes agleam,
As knotted chains become a dream.
She trips and sways, a sight to see,
That bling it moves, just like a bee!

Yet through the night, the joy remains,
With sparkles flying, like the rain.
In this riot of metal and beads,
A dance of folly is what she needs.

Prism of Hidden Stories

Glistening gems from days of yore,
Hold tales of love and even more.
They twinkle bright, with a cheeky grin,
Whispering secrets from deep within.

Once lost in boxes, they now prance,
In this lively, sparkling dance.
They jingle and chuckle as they roll,
Awakening stories from the soul.

Each jewel leaps with dance and glee,
A charm or two, quite boldly free.
And as they shine, the room ignites,
With laughter swirling, oh what sights!

A smack of brilliance, a flash of fun,
Together they twinkle, never to shun.
In this merry mix, they hold the key,
To a prism of joy, just wait and see!

The Charm of Twinkling Revelry

Upon her wrist, the bangles ring,
With every move, they dance and cling.
A clatter, a laugh, a merry sound,
Twinkling charms all around.

They roll and sway, in perfect time,
Creating rhythms, almost a rhyme.
In the spotlight, she spins with flair,
The charms giggle, floating in air.

A wink from a bracelet, a nudge from a ring,
Each glimmer adds to the joyful fling.
Her friends join in, what a delight,
A dazzling show, celebrating night!

With every clink, a story's told,
Of moments cherished and laughter bold.
In this twinkling revelry, we find,
A charm of joy, beautifully entwined.

Glistening Echoes of the Past

Whispers of gold in the twilight gleam,
Echoes of laughter, a shining dream.
With every sparkle, a giggle pings,
Old memories dance on glittering wings.

A brooch lost long, now found anew,
Winks and nods, like a playful crew.
They sway and twist as stories flow,
In this shiny realm, we put on a show.

Each piece a giggle, each clasp a tale,
Of fancy feasts and an ice cream trail.
They shimmer bright through thick and thin,
In a sparkly huddle, let the fun begin!

From tangled chains to a dazzling spin,
These echoes remind us of where we've been.
So here we frolic, with a wink and a dance,
Celebrating lives, as laughter's our chance.

Tides of Celestial Glamour

In the cupboard, jewels gleam bright,
Whispers of laughter take flight.
Sparkles tumble down like rain,
Wearing grandma's pearls, what a gain!

A hat too large, a shoe askew,
Twirl and swirl, what's a girl to do?
Dresses made of curtains, oh so grand,
As we prance in our own wonderland!

Mirror reflections, a comical sight,
Did I just trip? Oh, what a fright!
Giggles burst like bubbles in air,
Dramatic poses, we're quite the pair!

With each twirl, we defy the ground,
The room's a circus, laugh's the sound.
Glamour's just a game we play,
In this wacky, wonderful ballet!

Twilit Veils of Adoration

In twilight's glow, we cast a spell,
Wearing outfits that seem to yell.
Ruffles, bows, and mismatched stripes,
Dancing around like happy hype!

Feathers tickle, hats askew,
We laugh until we boo-hoo.
Gems made of plastic, shiny blue,
Nothing feels quite like this crew!

Pretending we're at royal balls,
Tripping over the kitchen stalls.
Twists and turns, oh what a feat,
Is that the dog's tail I just beat?

Twilit veils, we flutter near,
Chasing dreams without a fear.
In our fancy, funny parade,
Life's a stage where jokes are made!

Dance With the Embers of Elegance

Embers flicker, playful and bright,
Dressed in wonder, what a sight!
A tutu from last year's fair,
With mismatched socks, we're unaware!

Stepping lightly, grace all around,
In our minds, we're spellbound.
Sway like flames in a cozy breeze,
Giggling hard, we bend our knees!

A dance of grandeur, in the hall,
But wait, where's the cat? Oh, what a brawl!
With every leap, we leave a dent,
In this whimsical valiant event!

Embers glow as laughter grows,
Dancing lightly, strike a pose.
Elegance comes with fun and flair,
In the glow of moments we share!

Threads of Joy's Caress

Threads of joy weave bright arrays,
Worn in silly, unexpected ways.
Scarves wrapped too tight, hats bizarre,
In this magic, we shine like stars!

With every stitch, we tell a tale,
Of crazy moments, we shall regale.
Pants that gleam, a top that twirls,
In this gala where fun unfurls!

The cat struts like a fashion queen,
While we giggle behind the screen.
Each twirl spreads laughter, a funny sight,
In our whimsical world, everything's right!

Threads of joy, embrace the night,
In colors bright, pure delight.
Dancing in circles, so carefree,
These silly moments, just let them be!

A Fable of Finery

A girl adorned in shimmering flair,
Lost her charm in a royal air.
She twirled and laughed like a bright star,
Only to trip over her own bizarre.

Jewels clinked like clumsy bells,
As she danced near the wishing wells.
A wave turned into a confusing whirl,
Off flew a gem, oh what a swirl!

Gowns that sparkled, hats so grand,
Her style was more than what she planned.
But the laughter came from a sly grin,
For the treasures led to her playful spin.

In dreams of pearls, she'd often wallow,
Yet her dance left many to follow.
With every stumble became a new tale,
In the world of finery, she set sail.

Resplendent Illusions

In a cloak of gold, she made her bets,
Dancing past dignitaries and pets.
A twirl to impress, then a slip on the floor,
Oh, how they laughed and begged her for more!

Her jewels reflected the light of the sun,
But her footing was where the real fun was spun.
Each step a riddle, every sway a joke,
As luxurious dreams began to provoke.

With a whisk of her fan, she claimed the spotlight,
Yet tripped on her hem — oh, what a sight!
Crowds clapped and chortled at her grand spill,
As she danced on the edge of sheer thrill.

A mirage of glam, in laughter she shined,
For those who falter, get love from behind.
In the show of finesse, she's the queen of the jest,
For the finest of treasures belong to the best.

The Rhythm of Riches

With pockets of gold, she lightened the day,
Twirling full throttle, come what may.
Follies in heels, they'd leap and they'd bounce,
Fame struck a pose, they all would pronounce.

Around and around, like a merry-go-round,
Her riches were plentiful, laughter profound.
But mischief awaited whilst she played her part,
Wobbling and weaving, she danced from the heart.

A sparkle here, a twinkle there,
Richness of giggles spread through the air.
Even the crowns grew weary and light,
For a jest turned a ball into pure delight.

As she twirled away, she slipped with a grin,
The laughter erupted, oh where to begin?
In this rhythm of riches, all would agree,
It's the joys of the dance that are riches so free.

Echoing Elegance

Elegance echoed in the hall of dreams,
Dressed to the nines, or so it seems.
With a wiggle and jiggle, she burst into cheer,
Her gown took the lead, while her heels went near.

Each step a snicker, a playful parade,
As the elegance wobbled, her dignity frayed.
Like a duck in high heels, she quacked with delight,
These moments of pleasure made everything right.

Her crown took a tumble, jewelry aghast,
In this comical waltz, she felt unsurpassed.
The laughter cascaded, ringing through air,
Forget plumes of riches, it was fun beyond compare!

So here's to the mayhem, outrageous and grand,
To dance with abandon, nothing was planned.
Echoing elegance took flight like a kite,
In the world of the funny, her spirit ignites.

Threads of Infinite Grace

In a ball gown stitched with laughter's thread,
She twirls in circles, almost lost her head.
With every spin, a giggle spills bright,
As shoes fly off into the moonlit night.

A friend shouts loudly, 'Stop, you're too wild!'
But she swings like a carefree child.
Her hair's a whirl, like clouds gone astray,
Each step a promise of a new ballet.

A necklace shimmers, tales it can't confess,
While partners stumble, creating a mess.
In close encounters, they trip and they leap,
Oh, the joy of splendor, their laughter runs deep.

The night sails on, the moon starts to fade,
With each crazy twist, a new memory made.
Wrapped in the magic of fun and finesse,
They dance like dreams in a dazzling dress.

The Allure of Hidden Stories

Beneath grand chandeliers, whispers take flight,
An old tale shimmers in the dance's light.
She steps forward, confidence in her guise,
While he stumbles, lost in her sparkling eyes.

Gasp! A loose button leaps like a bird,
Landing boldly with a comedic word.
Laughter erupts like the pop of a cork,
As they spin stories in their fancy work.

Every costume hides secrets so bold,
In the folds of fabric, laughter unfolds.
From hidden pockets, sweets come alive,
With each shared treat, their spirits arrive.

With twinkling eyes, they navigate fate,
In a world where each moment's first-rate.
From whispers to giggles, they form a brigade,
Tales of sweet folly in masquerade.

Costume of Dreams

In a gown of fanciful fluff and delight,
She dances around, filled with sheer appetite.
With feathers that flutter and colors that shine,
Every turn she takes becomes quite the line.

A friend slips on sequins, parts of her dress,
Creating a flurry, oh what a mess!
They giggle and whirl, like leaves in the breeze,
Each twist a reminder to dance with such ease.

In the corner lurks a cat in her hat,
Judging the madness with a poised little pat.
Yet the shoes keep flying and spirits soar high,
In this costume of dreams, they aim for the sky.

As midnight beckons, they share a grand toast,
In laughter and chaos, they dance on the coast.
Oh, the joy woven into each hasty seam,
In the fabric of laughter, they fulfill each dream.

Twists of Fate

At a soirée filled with spirits so bright,
A pair of eyes sparkles, igniting the night.
With each charming smile, a twinkle of fun,
Their feet become tangled, a jig just begun.

A hapless fellow slips on spilled champagne,
As giggles erupt, he rewrites the game.
Twists and turns under the stars' kind gaze,
They dance on the edge of a whimsical craze.

His bow tie spins like a top gone astray,
While she laughs uproariously, brightening the fray.
In a whirl of silk and taffeta grace,
They find their own rhythm with comedic pace.

With little faux pas, they embrace every fate,
In this raucous reverie, they twirl and create.
A night full of stories that never feel late,
In laughter, they wander, it's simply first-rate.

Glimmers of Past Elegance

In a box on the shelf, it lay,
A glimmer of dreams that went astray.
Once adorned on a neck so fine,
Now a memory wrapped in twine.

Oh, the laughter that filled the room,
As friends gathered, chased away gloom.
But the sparkle now tells a lie,
For the threads are thin, and so am I!

With every clink and jingle sweet,
We'd dance as though life was a treat.
But beads can roll and fall away,
Just like the joy of yesterday.

Yet still it shines, that old delight,
With each twist, it twinkles bright.
What once was grace, now brings a grin,
At the silliness of what has been.

Chains of Desire

Upon my neck, a chain did sway,
A serpent of dreams that led me astray.
Each link a wish, a hopeful shout,
But beware the weight of jewels of doubt!

At parties, oh, how it would gleam,
Making me feel like a queen in a dream.
Yet, every glance brought a frown,
As I tripped and fell, all but crowned.

I waltzed with my burden, laughed till I cried,
My fancy trinket, my ego's pride.
But when it snapped on that dance floor grand,
I swirled like confetti, just as I planned!

Now hanging in shame, it tells a tale,
Of glitter and gold, and how I did fail.
Yet each clink still whispers fun from the past,
A chain of mistakes that forever will last.

The Lure of Opulence

Once a shining star of high class,
Flashing bling upon a sassy lass.
Its glamour drew the eyes so quick,
But it never could hide that it was a trick!

Caught in a whirlwind of shiny desire,
My heart was ablaze, fueled by fire.
As I twirled, it slipped, oh what a sight,
A waltzing tragedy in the moonlight!

Each bead went tumbling, a carnival game,
A parade of sparkle, gone wild, in shame.
But the laughter? Oh, it filled the air,
As jewels danced down without a care.

Now a jester in opulence's grasp,
With stories of blunders that make me gasp.
Yet in my missteps, there's joy to find,
For silliness sparkles far more refined.

Embers of Enchantment

A trinket that promised a magical night,
Danced on my neck, oh what a sight!
But the spell it cast had a twist so sly,
Sparkling dreams that made me sigh.

In the glow of the moon, it shimmered bright,
Turning my adventures to pure delight.
Yet at each little jig, it wobbled loose,
And I laughed as I searched, like a silly recluse!

The magic, it faded, as jewels fell free,
A cascade of laughter, just like me.
With every glance, the giggles would start,
For who knew that elegance could fall apart?

Now resting in shadows, a relic of fun,
It whispers of nights when we danced as one.
In the embers of joy that still brightly glow,
I find that enchantment, despite the show.

Threads of Transformation and Light

Once a trinket, oh so small,
Now a crown that steals the ball.
Hearts are racing, all in glee,
Wonders wrapped in jubilee.

An old string found in a shoe,
Turns to jewels with quite the view.
Laughter echoes, whirls about,
Who knew chaos could sprout?

Sparkle here, a twist or two,
Silently giggles break right through.
One little glance, one silly spin,
Whoa! Who invited that grin?

With every twirl, a story's spun,
Hidden quirks 'neath beams of fun.
In this realm where bright threads lie,
We dance, we laugh, we reach the sky.

Secrets Woven in Luminous Curves

In the dark, a shimmery plight,
Curves that laugh, twinkling bright.
Whispers flutter through the air,
Secrets waiting, unaware.

A little twist, a secret turn,
Underneath, the candles burn.
Bumps and giggles fill the night,
Luminous chaos, pure delight.

Found a glitter in my shoe,
Should I wear it? Yes, I do!
Crowds will chuckle, join the game,
Life's a sketch without a frame.

Woven tales from fabric light,
Bold and breezy, laughter's flight.
With every step, a riddle plays,
In glowing curves, we lose our ways.

Dance of the Dazzling Tresses

Tresses twirling, wild and free,
Grins and gasps, oh could it be?
A hairpin flung, a missing shoe,
The laughter spreads; we're not through!

Twist and shout, a folly's charm,
Playful knots, no cause for alarm.
Fanciful frolics, all in sync,
With every flip, we start to blink.

Glitter flies, it's pure delight,
Sparks ignite in cozy night.
Jumbled hair goes snip and snap,
This is how we share a laugh!

Dazzle, dazzle, step on toes,
Who's the fairest? Nobody knows!
In the mirror, reflection beams,
Crowning fun with crazy dreams.

Shadows That Wear Sparkle

Shadows shift, a mystery's cast,
Sprinkles twirl, oh what a blast!
Giggling whispers sway in time,
They dodge the light, their playful prime.

In the corner, a jeweled bow,
Hiding secrets, ready to show.
A silver wink, a teasing tease,
Watch them dance with utmost ease.

Fingers flick, a sparkle spill,
Laughter dances, gives a thrill.
Beneath the glint, the mischief lies,
In shadowy games, the fun never dies.

So come partake in this grand scheme,
Where shadows shine and moments gleam.
Joy's the crown, let's play the part,
With gleeful whispers that touch the heart.

Shadows in Shimmer

In a room of glimmering light,
Tiny jewels took to flight,
With a wink and a twirl,
They convinced the cat to whirl.

The chandelier shook with glee,
As pearls rolled off in spree,
The dog joined in, quite the sight,
Chasing sparkles left and right.

A hat fell down, all askew,
Dancing shoes lost a shoe,
The carpet joined in on the game,
Grasping all the frivolous fame.

Laughter echoed through the night,
As shadows joined the delight,
In a swirl of charm and jest,
They danced until they sank to rest.

Veils of Longing

Behind curtains, whispers play,
Bright adornments, come what may,
A feathered hat, oh so bold,
Wobbles on a head so old.

The mirror cracks with joy anew,
Reflecting charms of every hue,
A clumsy stumble steals the show,
As jewels tumble to and fro.

The laughs of friends are like a song,
As spoons are jiving all night long,
They chant, "Oh, come and see this mess!"
While spoons dance in glittery dress.

Amidst the chaos, spirits rise,
Chasing dreams under starry skies,
With every slip and every chance,
Life's a waltz, a silly dance.

Serpents of Light

Snakes in jewelry, quite the tease,
Slithering with the greatest ease,
They giggle as they twist and turn,
Their shiny scales begin to burn.

A rogue bangle joins the fray,
Dancing with a bit of sway,
While folks just sip their tea and sigh,
As a rogue necklace aims to fly.

With every spin and every twist,
The crowd can't help but laugh and list,
Some pearls fall off and start to roll,
Creating mayhem, that's their goal.

As laughter bursts like summer rain,
The serpents tease us once again,
In flashes bright and moments slick,
They charm us all, a parlor trick.

The Art of Radiance

Artful chaos in full bloom,
With rings adorned in every room,
They giggle as they take a spin,
While shadows coax the fun within.

A brooch that sparkles like the sun,
Leads the way in this silly run,
As hats and gloves join in the spree,
Creating art, so wild and free.

The laughter dances on the floor,
With bracelets clinking, begging more,
Each pendant sways, a joyful jest,
Inviting all to join the fest.

In a wild twirl, they culminate,
A jovial scene that's truly great,
In shimmering splendor, they do prance,
Together forming a dazzling dance.

Charm of the Shimmering Gaze

In a party dressed to impress,
With glimmers that shine, I confess,
A sparkle caught by surprise,
It winked with mischief in its eyes.

A neighbor tripped, his drink took flight,
A splash of red, oh what a sight!
My jewel twirled in the wild parade,
While laughter echoed, undelayed.

The chandeliers giggled, swung low,
As we danced to the rhythm's flow,
Each twinkling piece chimed in delight,
Making chaos feel so right.

With every twirl and every spin,
A story of joy, where to begin?
The shimmering gaze, a playful tease,
In moments like this, we live with ease.

Echoes of Ornamental Grace

A brooch on the floor, what a toss!
It danced around like a boss,
With every giggle, it soared so high,
Imagining it could fly.

My friend wore pearls with the greatest flair,
But tripped on their length—what a scare!
The laughter erupted, a joyous uproar,
As she ventured to search the floor.

Rings like confetti on fingers so bold,
They told wild tales, mischievous and old.
Each twinkle told stories of nights gone by,
When dreams and laughter were never shy.

An evening of charms, of grace in jest,
In a swirl of fabric, oh what a fest!
Ornamental echoes call us near,
As we dance on dreams and celestial cheer.

Lattice of Dreams and Trinkets

The lattice weaved with shining jewels,
Crafted by imaginative fools.
A mishmash of color, a riot of fun,
As we twirled under the golden sun.

A bracelet jingled, and away it flew,
How far would it go, would it find a new crew?
We laughed as it rolled, a rebellious ball,
In a treasure hunt, we would not stall.

With faux diamonds and charms of delight,
Each piece carried joy, shining bright.
The laughter bubbled like the finest brew,
Creating a night we'd hold true.

Amid the glitz, our friendship's bond,
In this web of trinkets, we proudly respond.
A tapestry woven of life's silly dreams,
Where laughter forever gleams.

Swaying in Gilded Hour

Under the stars in a gilded glow,
We twirled with a flair, not too slow.
The jewels bounced and swayed with glee,
As if the universe danced with me.

A tiara slipped, onto the floor it went,
While we giggled, our time well-spent.
Laughter rang like the sweetest tune,
As we whirled beneath the beaming moon.

Each jeweled trinket held a tale to tell,
Of mishaps and giggles, we knew so well.
In that gilded hour, we turned the night,
With whimsical dreams taking flight.

So here's to the shimmer and silly delight,
To friendships that sparkle and hold us tight.
In this swaying dance, we celebrate,
Life's treasured moments that won't wait.

Laces of Luxury

In a shop not far away,
A sparkly thing did giggle,
It wrapped around my neck with pride,
My wallet instantly did wiggle.

I twirled and spun, felt oh-so-fine,
But tripped on air, what a disaster!
The necklace flew, a gleaming swine,
It danced like a playful jester faster.

Friends laughed and stated with delight,
"That jewel must have a mind of its own!"
It sparkled bright in the moonlight,
While I lay there, all alone.

But with friends around, we chortled loud,
A dance-off broke, oh what a sight!
That necklace, once proud, drew in a crowd,
Turned our mishap into pure delight.

A Symphony of Sparkle

A shiny piece of something fine,
I slipped it on, felt like a queen,
But at the gala, I missed my sign,
And bumped a waiter—what a scene!

Glass clinked and laughter filled the air,
My necklace twinkled, oh so bright,
It swung and swayed without a care,
Accusing me of clumsy fright.

"Is it a dance, or are you shy?"
A friend chimed in with a cheeky grin,
While gems on my neck seemed to reply,
"Just watch us sparkle, let's begin!"

So I leaped and pranced, much to their glee,
The necklace twinkled like a star,
We laughed till our bellies ached with glee,
That night turned wild, yet bizarre.

Reflections of Radiance

In the mirror, a dazzler gleamed,
I twirled and preened, felt quite divine,
But then I noticed, oh, how I beamed,
A cough—a hairball, I must resign!

Down it dropped, that shiny slice,
With a clatter that echoed far and wide,
The cat thought it was quite a prize,
And from there, what a chase did slide!

Neighbors popped their heads out too,
"Are you part of the circus now?"
I laughed so hard, what else to do?
That naughty jewel took a bow.

So I collected, shining bright,
Amongst the chaos—a gleaming mess,
The laughter sparkled all that night,
In luxury's game, I felt truly blessed.

Charmed by Glistening

A shiny trinket I did find,
It whispered charms so sweet and bold,
But as I danced, 'twas not so kind,
I slapped my foot—oh, how it rolled!

It skittered right across the floor,
With every step, it giggled loud,
The crowd around began to roar,
As I slipped and felt quite proud.

"Is that jewelry or a pet?"
My friend yelled, tears of laughter streamed,
While I just wished I could forget,
To twirl and swoosh as I'd dreamed.

Yet with each mishap, joy took flight,
My pals joined in the gleeful race,
That charm of mine, oh what a sight,
Danced with laughter, kept up the pace.

Mirthful Jewels on the Verge

In a box so bright and grand,
A treasure found, not just a band.
Laughs and giggles fill the air,
As shiny gems begin to flare.

A bracelet tries to catch a wink,
Making faces, in a blink.
Earrings twirl with cheeky flair,
Winking at the ones who stare.

The ring spins like a playful cat,
Chasing after, a curious hat.
A sparkle here, a shimmer there,
Mirthful jewels, a lively pair.

As the party sways and swings,
All that glitters dances, sings.
With a chuckle and a glance,
These gems all love to prance!

Glowing Allure Under the Moon

Underneath the silver glow,
Diamonds giggle, putting on a show.
With every twinkle, tales unfold,
Laughter shared, a sight to behold.

Necklaces tangle in a jest,
Competing for who can be the best.
Bangles jingle with delight,
Joining in the joyous night!

The moonlight sparkles, eyes all wide,
As charms and gems begin to slide.
Rings roll off and start to play,
Chasing shadows 'til the day.

In this whimsical, twinkling spree,
Jewelry dances, wild and free.
With every laugh, they take a chance,
Under the glow, they waltz and prance!

Dancing Sparks of Timeless Splendor

Sparks of light begin to sway,
In a funny, joyous way.
Cameos laughing, lips rolled tight,
Beneath the stars, they share the night.

Brooches gossip as they shine,
Sharing secrets, oh so fine.
Chains that jingle, dance with pride,
Swaying together, side by side.

An opal tripped and laughed aloud,
Drawing in a curious crowd.
Everyone chuckled, but oh, the thrill,
As this party sparkled with good will!

Time unwinds with every twirl,
As beads and charms begin to whirl.
With a twist and a playful leap,
In this splendor, joy runs deep!

Symphony of Dazzling Desires

A symphony of sparkle plays,
All around, the laughter stays.
Gems are jiving, having fun,
Beneath the light of a glowing sun.

A pearl declared, "I'm the star!"
But a ruby laughed, "Not by far!"
Together they dance, claiming the floor,
With witty banter, who could want more?

The audience gasps at the sight,
As rings and gems whirl in delight.
With a glint and a giggle, they take the stage,
Creating joy like they're all the rage!

In this charmed and dazzling spree,
Desires twinkle, wild and free.
With every note, every chance,
They share their joy, and laugh, and dance!

Mystique of Reflections Held

In a shop so bright and bold,
Items gleamed, stories told.
A trinket here, a sparkle there,
Laughter echoes, fills the air.

Mirrors wink with every glance,
Shadows play, it's time to dance.
A twist, a turn, oh what a sight,
Gems and giggles, pure delight.

With each flicker, whispers flow,
'What's the price?' they want to know.
Coins are clinking, smiles abound,
While dizzy dreams spin all around.

As we swirl, the world's a play,
In this shimmer, we lose our way.
Estimates fly like butterflies,
Who knew shopping could bring such highs?

Harmonious Journey Through Light

A parade of sparkles roam,
Through aisles bright, they call it home.
Jingling laughter fills the space,
Chaos dressed in shining grace.

Each bauble tells a silly tale,
Of socks and spoons within the mail.
With every twist, the fun won't cease,
As bright ideas just increase.

They dangle, swing, with life so grand,
Twirling hearts in jeweled bands.
We chase reflections' silly jig,
And bump a wall, oh that's too big!

But who needs plans? We laugh instead,
With gems and giggles, we forge ahead.
In this adventure, we'll take a chance,
For laughter shines in every glance.

The Allure of Shining Dreams

In a market of dazzling light,
Gems wink gently, oh what a sight.
With every glance, our pockets ache,
As visions swirl, make no mistake.

Glistening treasures, shapes so odd,
That cheeky grin we can't applaud.
A brooch with eyes, it seems to know,
Just watch it wink — it steals the show!

A dance of bling and clever plays,
As friends all gawk, and pick displays.
Their glimmer calls, we take the bait,
In our quest for sparkles, oh so great!

And as we twirl, let laughter reign,
With a playful twist amidst the gain.
Each shiny charm our snickers tease,
In shimmering dreams, we find our ease.

Dance of the Midnight Spark

In evening light, the sparkles prance,
With silly steps, a playful dance.
Twinkling gems with a glowing grin,
Join the fun, let chaos begin.

They jig and jiggle without a care,
A wild party fills the air.
Neighbors peek with brows raised high,
'That shining gang, oh my, oh my!'

Laughter bounces, reflections swirl,
As each shiny piece begins to twirl.
With a wink and nod, the night unfolds,
In this circus of laughter, treasures bold.

So grab a gem, let humor shine,
In this dance, all hearts align.
For midnight sparkles never fade,
In our funny world, we find our trade.

Gems in the Moonlight

Under the moon, they shimmer bright,
Joking in sparkles, what a sight!
Dancing around like stars up high,
Gems giggle softly, oh my, oh my!

Each jewel boasts a tale to share,
Of late-night romps and silly flair.
With every twist and playful gleam,
They laugh at life, or so it seems!

On a velvet cloth, they spin and sway,
A playful band in the night's ballet.
Ruby joins in with a cheeky wink,
Sapphires jest while emeralds blink!

In the night's fun, they twirl and tease,
A jeweled party that aims to please.
Under the stars, their mischief rolls,
In this moonlit dance, they steal our souls!

Whispers of Adornment

Whispers of gems fill the air,
Making jokes without a care.
A diamond quips, "I'm hard to please,"
While pearls just giggle and toss the breeze.

Each charm's a jest, oh what a crew,
Gold laughs loudly, but silver's shy too.
In laughter's embrace, the jewels unite,
Spinning old tales until the moonlight.

The brooch, in a polka dot dress,
Claims she's the best in the fashion press.
With every nudge and playful poke,
Together they laugh, oh what a joke!

In this gathering of gleaming glee,
The night unfolds in hilarious spree.
With every twinkle, mischief's planned,
These jewels are tricky, oh so grand!

Elegance Entwined

Elegance winks in colors bright,
In a chandelier's glow, they take flight.
Witty whispers fill the clasp,
A pearl with sass, oh how they gasp!

In velvet night, they flirt and tease,
Emerald giggles bring hearts to ease.
With a sparkle, they dance along,
To the rhythm of a whimsical song!

A diamond declared, 'I've won the crown!'
While others jest and tumble down.
A ruby describes a clumsy fall,
As all the gems share laughter's call!

Beneath the stars, their stories blend,
In this charming ball, the fun won't end.
With every twirl and playful wink,
These gems remind us not to overthink!

A Twirl of Treasures

A treasure trove of laughter bright,
Dancing jewels catch the moonlight.
With blinks and nods, they take the floor,
In this gem-filled show, who could ask for more?

Spin around, they jive with glee,
"Look at me!" shouts the fancy key.
Diamonds chat about their shine,
While making jokes about the divine!

Glistening stones in a cheeky stance,
As each one shows off their best dance.
A sapphire shimmies with grace so spry,
While an old brooch just lets out a sigh!

With laughter echoed in the night,
These treasures twirl until the light.
In a whimsical show of sparkly flair,
They remind us all how joy is rare!

Illumination of Passionate Endeavors

In the market, bright and loud,
I spotted treasures, oh so proud.
A golden charm, a silly grin,
Thought I'd wear it, let the fun begin!

But as I twirled, it fell just right,
Into a puddle, oh what a sight!
With shimmer gone, my joy did fade,
I laughed it off, what a masquerade!

My phone rang out, a call to flee,
Chasing my dream like a busy bee.
Yet there it lay, my golden charm,
A tale of glee, its unmeant harm!

Who knew a charm could bring such bliss?
In puddles, gems can surely miss.
Still, I wear my laughter proud,
A quirky gem, I laugh aloud!

Circles of Luster and Lore

Under the moon, I pranced with glee,
Dressed in sparkles, just like a bee.
Each twirl and twist flung shine in the air,
Till my shoe caught on not-so-cool hair!

I stumbled round, my friends did cheer,
While I flailed about without a fear.
Each swish and swirl, a dance gone wrong,
But oh, the laughter kept us strong!

"Look at her!" they'd giggle with delight,
Spinning like a top, what a silly sight!
In circles we danced, both joy and jest,
Creating tales we would never rest!

The night grew dim, yet we shone bright,
In circles of laughter, pure delight.
With lore of mishaps, we'd always share,
Sassy adventures, without a care!

Tangle of Radiant Vows

Adorned in jewels, a grand display,
I made a promise to dance today.
But a tangle of beads caught in my hair,
Had me looking like a sparkly bear!

With friends around, I gave it a yank,
Jewel from hair, but lost my prank.
A lasso of laughter, we twirled anew,
In radiant vows, just me and my crew.

We flopped and flailed, a comedic spree,
Each twist yielding more to see.
Gems on our heads, a riotous sight,
In tangled laughs, we danced through the night!

Though beads did scatter, we held our ground,
In joyous rebellion, our joy was found.
With radiant vows of friendship true,
We tangled in laughter, just me and you!

Crescendos of Delicate Beauty

As the music played, I took a stance,
With a flourish, I began to prance.
But a slip on the floor made all gone awry,
I ended up flat, with a muffled cry!

Crescendos of laughter rose all around,
While I wriggled like a worm on the ground.
In a flurry of giggles, I joined the fest,
A delicate beauty, at its humorous best!

Over my head, a glimmering light,
A chandelier swinging, what a fright!
Down it came with a glint and a clang,
But I took my bow, just let the fun hang!

So we danced and we laughed, all in good cheer,
Embracing the bloopers that brought us near.
With crescendos of joy, we swayed and we spun,
In a hilarious tale, we were all the one!

www.ingramcontent.com/pod-product-compliance
Lightning Source LLC
Chambersburg PA
CBHW070325120526
44590CB00017B/2821